Venus Williams

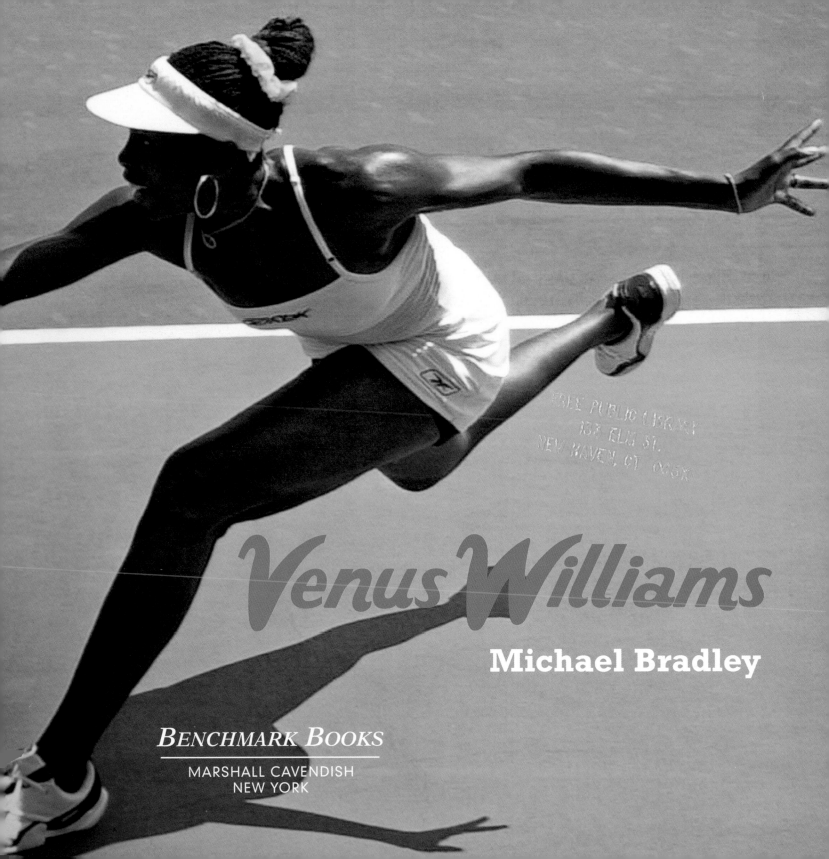

Venus Williams

Michael Bradley

BENCHMARK BOOKS

MARSHALL CAVENDISH
NEW YORK

Benchmark Books
Marshall Cavendish
99 White Plains Road
Tarrytown, NY 10591-9001
www.marshallcavendish.com

Library of Congress Cataloging-in-Publication Data

Bradley, Michael, 1962-
  Venus Williams / by Michael Bradley.
    p. cm. — (Benchmark all-stars)
Includes bibliographical references and index.
Contents: The world is watching — Humble beginnings — Getting started
— Starts and stops — The big time — Number one.
  ISBN 0-7614-1630-7
  1. Williams, Venus, 1980—-Juvenile literature. 2. Tennis
players—United States—Biography—Juvenile literature. 3. African
American women tennis players—Biography—Juvenile literature. [1.
Williams, Venus, 1980- 2. Tennis players. 3. African
Americans—Biography. 4. Women—Biography.] I. Title II. Series:
Bradley, Michael, 1962- . Benchmark all-stars.

  GV994.W49B73 2003
  796.342'092—dc21

2003007087

Photo research by Regina Flanagan.

Cover: Yassukovich/Corbis Sygma
AP/Wide World Photos: 2–3, 8, 10, 11, 12, 14, 15, 22, 24, 28, 29, 33, 34, 39 (left);
Manny Millan/SI/Icon Sports Media: 6, 16; Duomo/Corbis: 9 (left), 42; Craig
Ambrosio/Icon Sports Media: 9 (right); Preston Mack/Icon Sports Media: 17; Roncen
Patrick/Corbis Kipa: 18; Susan Mullane/Icon Sports Media: 20; S. Carmona/Corbis: 27;
Icon Sports Media: 30; AFP/Corbis: 32, 35, 36, 38, 39 (right).

Series design by Becky Terhune

Printed in Italy
1 3 5 6 4 2

Contents

Venus Williams poses with her sister Serena Williams after winning the 2001 U.S. Open championship.

CHAPTER ONE
The World Is Watching

It was a dream come true. For years, Richard and Oracene Williams had hoped that their two daughters would play against each other in New York for the U.S. Open title. There, on the world's brightest tennis stage, their family would *reign* supreme. And now it was happening. In September 2001, Venus and Serena Williams took the court at Arthur Ashe Stadium in Queens, New York, and made history. For the first time since 1884—yes, 1884—sisters would be playing for a major tennis title. And, perhaps more importantly, two African-American sisters would be competing for the championship. This was big. Really big. CBS broadcast the match on prime-time television on a Saturday night. The nation's media was buzzing. Celebrities were out to watch the magic. Everybody wanted to watch the Williams Sisters Show.

"Basically, it was my dad's dream, my mom's dream," Venus said. "They told us we'd be here, playing each other in the finals. That's why we believed it. If they had told us we would never make it playing tennis, I don't think we'd be here today."

Ever since Richard Williams had seen how much prize money and endorsement money successful female tennis players could make, he had pledged to help any daughter of his

Defending Wimbledon champ Venus Williams returns a shot by Virginia Ruano Pascual of Spain in the 2002 Wimbledon tournament.

become a star in the sport (there are five Williams sisters: Yetunde, Isha, Lyndrea, Venus, and Serena.) So, when Venus Ebone Starr Williams was born in 1980 he started her on the road to stardom. When Venus beat Serena, 6–2, 6–4, to win the 2001 Open, it was clear that he had reached his goal. Venus had won her fourth major tournament and her second of the year. (She had also taken Wimbledon.) By the beginning of 2002, Venus would be ranked number one in the world. The 6'1", 170-pound Venus with the blazing serve (it had been clocked at 128 miles per hour) and the powerful strokes was on top. So was the Williams family.

But that didn't mean things would change between the sisters. They were still extremely close. Best friends. After Venus won the match, she hugged her younger sister Serena at the net. "I love you, all right?" she asked. The match had been big, but family was the most important thing. It always had been and always would be. "I take care of Serena," Venus said. "I make sure she has everything, even if I don't have anything. I love her."

The road had never been easy. Many people had criticized Richard Williams for his methods. He had pulled the girls out of California's junior tennis program and moved them to Florida. There, they had trained by themselves and had not played in any tournaments. When Venus finally made her debut on the *professional circuit*, she was seen by

Venus Williams hugs her sister after beating her in the 2001 U.S. Open championship match.

Venus Williams prepares for a backhand return against Amanda Coetzer in the 2002 NASDAQ-100 Open in Miami.

some as a victim of her father's dreams and schemes. Even as she was winning the 2001 U.S. Open, the critics continued to take their shots. She was rude, some said. Others wondered whether the family had "fixed" the matches between Venus and Serena, deciding ahead of time which sister should win. Through it all, Venus and Serena stayed close to each other, trying to keep their bond strong—on and off the court.

"This is our first Grand Slam title together, and that's the way we'd like to be, because both of us win, in a way," Venus said. "Also, I just don't like to see [that] Serena [has] lost against anybody—even me. I don't exactly feel like I won. If I was playing a different opponent, I would probably be a lot more joyful."

Venus Williams has been pretty happy since she turned professional in October 1994. She has become a dominant force on the women's tennis tour, able to overpower opponents with her strength, conditioning, and determination. She has amassed more than $10 million in prize money and

Despite her success and all the attention that goes with it, Venus Williams remains friendly and fun-loving.

won twenty-nine singles championships during her professional career. And even though 2002 wasn't her best year—she won seven tournaments but lost to Serena in the finals of three majors—she remains one of the world's best. But Venus Williams has been a phenomenon since she was just a child. *The New York Times* featured her on its front page when she was only ten years old. Even then, people knew she was a special talent.

Now, everyone knows. Venus and Serena Williams have fulfilled their father's *prediction* that his daughters would become the biggest sensations in women's tennis.

"No one seemed to enjoy our comments, and people were pretty *cynical*," Venus said. "But we're showing that we're capable of doing what we always said we could."

Venus is more than just a tennis player. She is committed to education, and travels with a laptop that links her to classes in fashion design.

She has earned a certificate in interior decorating and started her own interior design firm (V Starr Interiors), and is studying for her bachelor's degree in design. She loves to read. She enjoys learning about new cultures and attempting to master foreign languages. Thanks to her appeal to marketers, Venus has begun to learn about the business world through her many endorsements. And for someone who is still so young, just imagine what is ahead of her in life and on the courts.

"I'm not sure if we quite understand how much we do for the game," Venus said. "We just are trying to do our best for ourselves. We're trying to get some Grand Slam [titles] under our belts."

Getting Grand Slams isn't the question. The question is, how many?

Venus Williams has never forgotten her roots in youth tennis. Here, she gives instruction to inner-city children in Boston.

CHAPTER TWO
Humble Beginnings

Richard Williams had no formal tennis training. There weren't too many courts near the cotton fields where he grew up in Shreveport, Louisiana. He didn't have much of a traditional education, either. Williams dropped out of school at age sixteen to earn money to help his family. None of that would stop him. Williams was a determined man with a dream.

From the moment Richard Williams saw professional tennis player Virginia Ruzici earn $30,000 for winning the French Open on June 11, 1978, he knew he wanted Venus and Serena to play tennis. To become stars. To dominate the sport. So he taught himself the game. At the time, he and his family were living in Compton, California, where violent gangs are everywhere, but hitting a yellow ball over a net isn't too common. Still, there he was, in 1984, packing six rackets, seven milk crates full of tennis balls, and four-year-old Venus into a Volkswagen van. They went to the beat-up courts in poor areas to practice. And practice. And practice.

"We play on two courts," Richard Williams once said. "That's all there is—and they look like trash, they're so slippery."

Richard Williams congratulates his daughter after she won the 2001 Ericsson Open—but her winning was no surprise. After all, she had won against John McEnroe as a child.

Despite the poor conditions, Venus developed quickly. By the time she was eight, tennis legend John McEnroe and then-champion Pete Sampras were watching her play. Venus had graduated from the sometimes uneven and slippery public courts to a well-groomed *surface* in Brentwood, California. McEnroe even played against her. And when her father told Venus that McEnroe—the onetime number one men's player—had held back to let her win, she didn't believe him. "She told me she thought she could have beaten him," Williams said.

It wasn't all good times for Venus. Even though she was hugely successful on the southern California junior tennis circuit, Richard didn't think it was good for her. Other parents took it too seriously. He tried to get Venus to quit the game. Perhaps she could concentrate on track, where she was also enjoying great success. She was undefeated in nineteen meets and was a budding star in the mile run. (She ran the distance in five minutes twenty-nine seconds at age eight.) No chance. Venus stopped track instead. She wanted to be a tennis player.

By the time Venus was eleven years old, she was ranked number one among girls twelve-and-under in southern California. Her younger sister, Serena, was the top talent in the ten-and-under division. But Richard Williams was sick of the junior tennis scene. The

> **When her father told Venus that McEnroe— the onetime number one men's player—had held back to let her win, she didn't believe him. "She told me she thought she could have beaten him."**
>
> **—Richard Willams**

parents in the division were too competitive and put too much pressure on their children. He pulled the sisters off the circuit and moved the whole family to Florida.

It didn't matter that many observers were predicting stardom for Venus and Serena. He didn't care that famous boxing promoter Don King was interested in helping the girls make the big time. Richard Williams was ready for a change.

"It was tough to accept change," Venus admitted years later. "I don't like it in the supermarket, when they change the position of something when they put it in another aisle. I get upset. When people saw that we didn't play junior tennis, it was out of the ordinary, and they said, 'They will never make it.'"

Richard Williams heard the whispers. He knew people thought he had made a mistake. Taking the girls out of competitive tennis would never prepare them for the professional tour. But family came first for him. He feared the cutthroat atmosphere of the junior circuit would crack the bond he had built for the family. The girls had become closer than most sisters. Serena remembers them having

Venus Williams played in only four tournaments as a fifteen-year-old, but still attracted plenty of attention.

After winning the 2001 U.S. Open, Venus Williams (left) exchanges a smile with her sister during the awards ceremony.

their last fight when she was six years old. "Family comes first," she said. "Nothing will come between me and my sister."

While Venus and Serena's father managed the girls' careers, their mother, Oracene, taught them how to be strong women. Strong black women. She taught them that there would be *prejudice* and jealousy, but words couldn't hurt them. Oracene Williams was helping Venus and Serena prepare for the world of professional tennis, which can be extremely *petty*. She wanted the girls to know they were special, and not just because they could hit a tennis ball well. Richard Williams brought his family to Delray Beach, Florida, and enrolled the girls in Rick Macci's tennis academy. There, Venus received her first professional instruction. Yes, Williams had worked hard to learn the game and to teach it to his daughters, but there was no substitute for experience. Under the hot Florida sun, Venus went to work. "Six hours a day, six days a week for four years," Macci says. "There wasn't a day that the girl

Mama's girls: Venus Williams (left) and Serena Williams (right) smile for the camera with their mother, Oracene Williams, in 2002.

wouldn't hit two hundred serves." It was in Florida that Venus polished her skills. She was away from the spotlight. Away from the critics. Away from the competition. Some figured it would ruin her chances of major success.

They were about to find out just how wrong they were.

Venus Williams's beaded hairstyles were hot topics of conversation when she made her debut on the women's tour.

CHAPTER THREE

Getting Started

*V*enus's professional career was all of two matches old when Richard Williams made his move. Rick Macci, at whose Florida-based tennis academy Venus and Serena had trained for four years, had advised Williams to make an endorsement deal with a shoe company before Venus played a match on the Women's Tennis Association (WTA) tour. So had family legal adviser Keven Davis. Instead, Williams took the family to Disney World to break the tension.

The advice was right. If Williams had cut a deal and Venus had struggled as a professional, there would still be a guarantee of some money. But Williams had his own plan—as always. He believed in his daughter and thought the best way to attract the Nike and Reebok shoe companies of the world would be for her to play. And win.

"I thought he was taking a serious gamble," Davis said. "He proved us all wrong."

So, on October 31, 1994, fourteen-year-old Venus took to the court in Oakland, California, against Shaun Stafford in the Bank of the West Classic. And she won. In the second round, Venus took a 6–3, 3–1 lead over then-power Arantxa Sanchez-Vicario before wilting and losing the next eleven games. Still, it was a dramatic—and successful—

After devoting so much time and effort to his children's careers, Richard Williams can now relax and enjoy their games.

debut. Afterward, when the media asked Venus about how the loss to Sanchez-Vicario compared to her previous defeats, she struggled for an answer. It wasn't a tough question. It was just that she had never lost a match before.

Venus's performance in Oakland created exactly the kind of attention Richard Williams had predicted. All of a sudden, Venus was a hot commodity. The big shoe and apparel companies all wanted her. Seven months later, without having played in another professional *tournament*, Venus cashed in. She signed a five-year, $12-million deal with Reebok. It was an unprecedented amount of money for someone so young. Venus couldn't even boast about her successes on the junior circuit, because she hadn't played on it. But there it was. Richard Williams's gamble had paid off.

The four years in Florida had been just what Richard and Oracene Williams wanted for their family. Venus and Serena had trained hard. They had played in *exhibition matches*. At one point, Serena had teamed with the legendary Billie Jean King in a *doubles competition* against Venus and Rosie Casals, another former great. King had been impressed, but she had offered some wise counsel. "The important thing is that they go slowly and do the right thing," she had said. "That's what makes champions."

Macci insisted that Richard Williams was doing it right. Sure, the father and the coach had some battles. Williams could say and do some strange things at times. (He once said at a press conference that he was seeking to buy New York City's Rockefeller Center for $3.8 billion.) But the girls' welfare was his main concern.

"Richard and I had ups and downs over a lot of things, but he's always been an incredible father to those two girls," Macci said. "If he'd wanted more money, he could've had them playing more. But I can remember fifty times when he called off practice because Venus's grades were down. They'd be in my office studying French, and I'd be saying, 'Hey, we've got to work.'"

The girls' off-court results were just as impressive as their powerful ground strokes. Both graduated with 3.0 averages from the Driftwood Academy, a private school in Lake Park, Florida, that caters to students with unconventional lives. Venus studied French and German. She wrote poetry and wanted to study fashion design. Though her life was completely different from the ordinary teenager's, Venus wasn't living just to hit the ball.

When she did get on the court, Venus was proving that she belonged. Though still a teenager, she was

Wimbledon

Although there are many prestigious tennis tournaments each year, none can match the spectacle and tradition of Wimbledon.

Played over a three-week period in June and early July at the All England Lawn and Tennis Club in the London suburb of Wimbledon, the tournament blends the refined English culture with the sport's most talented performers, who tangle on the club's grass courts. A member of the British royal family is almost always in attendance at the tournament's more important matches, and the cream of English society turns out for the competition. Even the refreshments offered at concession stands have a distinct English flavor. At what other sporting event can you get strawberries and cream?

The final matches are played at Centre Court before a packed house and a worldwide television audience. The champions receive silver platters as trophies.

When she played at Wimbledon in 1997, Venus Williams braided her hair with purple and green beads, the official Wimbledon colors.

making progress. She advanced to the third round of the Lipton Championships in Florida in March 1997—not bad for a seventeen-year-old. But it was there that she began to experience some jealousy and *animosity* from other players. After Venus lost to Martina Hingis in the Lipton Championship, an official gave Hingis one of the 1,800 beads that had been in Venus's hair. Hingis threw it to the press, saying, "I have a present for you: one of Venus's pearls." Although the gesture wasn't a true snub, it showed that some members of the women's tennis community weren't that impressed with Venus—and weren't rooting for her to succeed.

If that was the case, those folks must have been happy three months later. On June 28,

1997, Venus made her English debut at Wimbledon, tennis's grandest stage. It wasn't pretty. She lost to ninety-first-ranked Magdalena Grzybowska of Poland, hardly a powerhouse, in the first round. The British papers were breathless. "VENUS OUT OF ORBIT," one headline screamed. Venus, on the other hand, wasn't worried. "It's my first Wimbledon," she said. "There will be many more."

A few months later, in September at the U.S. Open, Venus more than atoned for her Wimbledon trouble. She became the first unranked women's finalist, rocketing through the matches, playing exciting tennis. Of course there was some *controversy*. During a semifinal match, opponent Irina Spirlea intentionally bumped Venus during a changeover. Richard Williams claimed Spirlea used a racial slur. The incident received huge media attention. Meanwhile, Venus was showing the world what lay ahead. The U.S. Open finals at age seventeen. What could be next?

As it turned out, plenty.

CHAPTER FOUR
Starts and Stops

Venus's star was rising, and that meant more money and more success. It also meant more attention. She was no longer just a prospect. After her U.S. Open run, Venus was the talk of women's tennis. How could this seventeen-year-old have turned the tour on its ear in one tournament? She had done it, and all of a sudden, people were trying to learn more about her. They were trying to figure her out. Because she was African American in a sport dominated by white players, Venus attracted more notice than some other prodigies. Some even compared her to golf superstar Tiger Woods.

"I would hope so," Venus said. "He's different from the *mainstream*, and in tennis I also am. I'm tall. I'm black. Everything's different about me. Just face the facts."

The 1997 U.S. Open was the first played in the brand-new Arthur Ashe Stadium, named for the great African-American player. But that didn't prevent some resentment about Venus's race. By the end of the tournament, there were as many questions about racism in tennis as about rocketing serves and powerful ground strokes. Even Martina Hingis, who beat Venus, 6–0, 6–4, in the final and was no fan of the Williams family, saw that things had *deteriorated*. "It was a little mess," she said. "Like a boxing fight at the end."

The Women's Tennis Association—which governs the major players on the women's professional tour—handles the rankings of its members in two ways.

The first is an overall ranking. Throughout the year, players are measured by how they do in various tournaments. If a competition is won, the ranking goes up, particularly if it is one of the "majors." A player's ranking also depends on the level of competition she faces and how she fares. If a player is highly ranked, the ranking of the player who beats her will rise more than if the first player ranked lower. The final rankings are computed at the end of the season. That means that players who win big later in the year can improve their standings at the end of the season.

The other way to rank players is by tournament. This is called *seeding the field*. Before each competition begins, organizers determine the order in which they think the players will finish. The top seed is expected to have the best chance to win. But the seedings aren't just calculated according to the rankings. Organizers also consider how a player does on a certain surface. For instance, a player who excels on grass but doesn't play well on clay wouldn't be a high seed at the French Open, which is played on clay. Also, how a person has done before can matter. A player who has always performed well at Wimbledon might get a higher seed than her ranking would indicate she deserves. A good seeding in a tournament is important, since higher seeds face more lightly regarded foes in earlier rounds and get a clearer path to the semifinals and finals.

The tennis community wasn't too happy with the whole Williams family. They weren't comfortable around Venus and Serena, who seemed to be in their own world when together. Many were angry with Richard Williams, who came to the sisters' matches with large signs that shouted encouragement but also proclaimed the Williams's success. Venus wasn't about to change that. She had been brought up to be successful. Her older sisters—Yetunde, Isha, and Lyndrea—were all thriving in college and had big plans. They had been taught by their parents that anything was possible. Their lives might have begun in poverty, but their futures were as bright as or brighter than those of others who had grown up in luxury. "Most of all, we do our own thing," Venus said. "We do what we want. We're very different from everyone else, because we think differently."

Though Venus Williams was moving up the rankings (her 1997 U.S. Open performance took her from sixty-sixth to twenty-seventh place), she wasn't perfect. There were some potholes on her golden road to success. In 1998, she advanced to the quarterfinals at Wimbledon against Jana Novotna. Venus was winning the match handily when she became upset after some line calls didn't go her way. Instead of rallying, Venus fell apart. "Why is this happening?"

she asked. She lost. Early the next year, she had more trouble, this time at the Australian Open. When some beads fell from her hair and onto the court during play against Lindsay Davenport, Venus was assessed a penalty point. It was a rare move by the referee, but the rules called for such a punishment. The incident rattled Venus, and she didn't win another game in the match.

Many felt Venus had cracked under pressure, and it is fair to say that she didn't handle the trouble well. But Oracene Williams didn't believe that. She felt her daughters' upbringing and their African-American status prepared them well for tough situations. "There's no such thing as pressure," Oracene Williams said. "As black Americans, that's all we've ever had. It's life. So, where's the pressure?"

Despite those problems, Venus

Venus Williams prepares to serve during the 1997 U.S. Open.

Williams celebrates after beating number-one-ranked Martina Hingis at the 1998 International in Australia.

was becoming a tennis star. She proved that during 1998 when she moved into the top ten, following her win at the Lipton Championship. That represented a jump of more than one hundred spots in just a year. She also won the IGA Invitational, reached the finals in the Italian Open and the Adidas International, and was a quarterfinalist at the French Open. She teamed with Serena to win the doubles title at the IGA, and won the mixed-doubles crown in Australia with Justin Gimelstob.

Venus did it with an intimidating serve and a variety of powerful strokes. She could pound the ball with the best along the baseline, or charge the net and put away winners. Her size and athletic ability were rare on the women's circuit, and some of her opponents were frightened to play against her. She and Serena represented a new wave of tennis player.

Yes!!! After winning an important point against Spain's Arantxa Sanchez-Vicario at the 1998 U.S. Open, Venus Williams shows her excitement.

"There's no such thing as pressure. As black Americans, that's all we've ever had. It's life. So, where's the pressure?"
—Oracene Williams

They were not only well-schooled in the fundamentals, but also capable of unleashing a rare combination of speed and athletic ability.

"Sometimes, I'm in awe," Irina Spirlea said. "They have something the others don't have."

Hingis's assessment was more to the point: "They're the strongest opponents on the tour." In 1999, Venus's strength was in evidence in many ways.

Venus (left) and Serena Williams share a
friendly moment during the October 1999
U.S. Open at Flushing Meadow, New York,
where they competed against each other.

CHAPTER FIVE
The Big Time

It was a landmark event. For the first time in 115 years, two sisters would be meeting in a championship final. Richard Williams knew it was a big deal. Before the match, he stood up in his section at the Lipton Championships and held up a sign. It read: "WELCOME TO THE WILLIAMS SHOW." That's exactly what it was. Venus and Serena would be squaring off for the title.

It was a big moment in tennis history, and it was not without tension. How would Richard Williams, who had nurtured both his daughters to be champions, handle the pressure? It wasn't easy.

"I really thought I was going to cry," he said afterward. "What was going through my mind was all the problems we've had in tennis, bringing the girls up, how difficult it was, the gang members, all the people out there.

"I was saying, 'Look where you are today.' It was so difficult for me to believe."

Difficult, but real. Venus took the first set, 6–1, and went on to a 4–3 lead in the second before Serena won four straight games to even the match. In the end, Venus was too much for her younger sister and she closed out the win with a 6–4 third-set triumph.

Venus and Serena Williams don't just play against each other. They are also a formidable doubles team. Here they take a moment to chat during their doubles match at the 1999 Australian Open.

Some thought the sisters plotted to have the match go three sets, in order to create greater television exposure. Richard Williams denied it. So did Venus. "Serena always comes back and beats people," she said. "I didn't want to become another victim. It was all I could do to hold her off."

When it was over, Venus went to the net and gave her sister a high-five. There wasn't a celebration. Venus and Serena walked off the court together, happy to have survived their first championship meeting. It wouldn't be their last.

"It's not too big," Venus said about the event. "In the end, we go home; we live life. You have to be happy after that. You have to remind yourself it's a game, and there's only one winner. Next week, there will be another opportunity."

And more success. Before 1999 was half over, Venus had four victories, including a win against Mary Pierce in the Italian Open final. That gave Venus two titles in two weeks. She was ranked fifth in the world, and she was on a roll. "I like being the best," Venus said. She wasn't bragging. Though only nineteen years old, she was rolling through the tennis world, winning

Tennis legend Billie Jean King passes on a few pointers to Venus Williams before the Federation Cup match in 1999.

Venus Williams just can't help winning. Here she hits the ball and wins the match against Amanda Coetzer of South Africa, during the 1999 WTA Tournament match in Hamburg, Germany.

events and attracting attention. When she and Serena helped the United States win the Federation Cup—an international competition involving head-to-head matches between different countries—in the fall of 1999, team captain Billie Jean King was impressed.

"Venus is working on her game and trying different things, which takes a lot of courage," King said. "She's very open to change."

That included her life off the court. Once she completed her high-school diploma work, Venus looked forward. She started pursuing a fashion-design degree. She was working on psychology and English composition courses, too. Critics thought she was living a sheltered life, just playing tennis and studying. They wanted her to get out, to date and socialize more. Venus wasn't having any of it. She would decide what happened.

"I do exactly what I want to do, and what I want to do is play tennis," she said. "I decided I

"Serena always comes back and beats people. I didn't want to become another victim. It was all I could do to hold her off."
—Venus Williams

wanted to go to school in the fall, and I made room for that. If I find there is anything else I want to do, I will make sure I do it."

One thing on her to-do list was to win a major championship. Although she had made it to the 1997 U.S. Open final, Venus had not been close to a title of that magnitude since. In 1999, she had her shot when she met Martina Hingis, her longtime rival, in the U.S. Open semifinal. It was a classic slugfest, with both players making great shots. In the end, however, Venus lost a three-set decision. Meanwhile, Serena won the family's first major, when she defeated Hingis in the final. For that moment, it appeared as if the little sister had passed her older sibling. People who had predicted great things for Venus were now praising Serena.

"I had reached an all-time low," Venus said. "It was a match I just gave away. I said to myself, 'Venus, what more could you do wrong?' I had no other options. It was either stay a *mediocre* player or move forward."

In the next two years, Venus would be on top of the tennis world. The loss at the 1999 U.S. Open had been tough, but she was tougher.

Venus Williams holds her trophy and smiles with happiness after winning the Italian Open in May 1999.

Sheer happiness: Venus Williams hugs the silver platter given as first prize to the winner of the 2000 Wimbledon singles tournament.

CHAPTER SIX
Number One

When she finally reached the summit, in late February 2002, Venus could have looked down on everyone else in women's tennis. Instead, she chose to honor the past. It was official. Venus was the first African American to be ranked number one in either the men's or the women's game. But since the rankings hadn't started until 1975, Venus knew she wasn't the true trailblazer. That distinction went to Althea Gibson, who had played in the 1950s and was one of the greatest ever. "It would be foolish to forget Althea Gibson," Venus said. "She was the first. And more than anything, I just feel proud to represent America in my sport."

The more than two years following Venus's 1999 U.S. Open semifinal loss to Martina Hingis had been enough to make anyone proud. Venus had won Wimbledon and had twice won the U.S. Open. That had not only ended her major title drought, it had drowned it out. Venus had become a dominant player and had swept numerous titles all over the world. Her number one ranking was not only appropriate; it was inevitable.

The ride to the top started in an odd fashion. Early in 2000, Richard Williams joined Venus at the Ericsson Open in Key Biscayne, Florida, and announced that he wanted his

Venus Williams raises the U.S. Open trophy aloft after winning the 2000 tournament.

daughter to retire. True, Venus was struggling, and tendinitis in her wrist wasn't helping, but there was no way she was quitting. This was just one more twist in a wild journey. "My life has been a saga," she said.

By July, that story was getting happier by the day. Despite having played only nine matches all year, Venus went to Wimbledon and won the ladies' tournament. By playing a much more aggressive game and charging the net more than ever, Venus trampled all comers. She even whipped her sister Serena in the semifinals, although it wasn't a win she could enjoy. Her straight-sets final triumph over rival Martina Hingis was a different story. Venus danced with glee. Her father boogied in the stands. It was a great moment, one that Venus no doubt cherished. She was happy on all fronts now, and that helped her play better tennis.

"I love winning Wimbledon," she said. "I love playing tennis. I love winning titles. And I realized I wouldn't be any happier in my life in general if I won or lost. Sure, in the tennis part of my life, I'd be much happier. But winning, losing, money, riches, or fame doesn't make you happy. For my tennis career, this is great. But as far as being Venus, it doesn't really make a huge difference."

It got even better being Venus in September 2000, when she added the U.S. Open title to her resume. Once again, her finals victim was Lindsay Davenport, whom she thrashed in straight sets. The trophy would bear the names of both Williams sisters, because they had won back-to-back titles. That was the most rewarding thing for Venus, who despite her budding independence was still extremely close to Serena. There was still more to love about 2000 for Venus.

Venus and Serena Williams embrace after winning the gold medal in women's doubles at the 2000 Summer Olympics in Sydney, Australia.

Venus Williams jumps for joy after defeating Lindsay Davenport to win the 2000 singles title at Wimbledon.

That same September, she won the Olympic gold in women's singles in Australia, and teamed with Serena to take the doubles title.

"To have a victory like this with Serena, my sister, a family member, my best friend, doesn't happen very often," Venus said of the Olympic triumph. "It's very rare. Just to be able to stand up together and succeed together on this level has been really, really good."

When the year was over, Venus had won thirty-five *consecutive* singles matches and was threatening to take over women's

Arthur Ashe

There have been several successful African-American tennis performers, but none made the impact that Arthur Ashe did. He played at a time when the sport had some of its most talented and successful players, giants of the sport like Sweden's Bjorn Borg, Australia's Rod Laver, and Jimmy Connors and John McEnroe of the United States.

In 1975 Ashe became the first African-American male to win the Wimbledon singles title. (Althea Gibson was the first African-American female champion, in 1957. She also won in 1958.) Ashe was also the 1968 U.S. Open champion. But his influence extended well beyond his victories. Ashe was a man of great dignity, who moved smoothly within the tennis world while speaking out for the rights of African Americans within the sport and throughout the United States. He was also an outspoken opponent of racism in South Africa in the days of apartheid—a policy that kept black and white South Africans separate.

When Ashe died, in 1993, after a long battle with many health problems, the American sporting scene lost one of its greatest ambassadors.

tennis. What made the victories even sweeter was a $40-million endorsement deal with Reebok, the largest-ever for a female athlete. A year that had begun with so much uncertainty had ended with tremendous prosperity. "No one would have thought that out of nowhere, after an injury, Venus would come back and play like she did," Davenport said.

The question as 2001 dawned was whether Venus could do it again. The answer was a resounding yes! She defended her Wimbledon crown and then headed to the U.S. Open to battle the world—and Serena. When she had finished, Venus had her second straight U.S. Open crown, to go with dual Wimbledon championships. It was a huge moment for Venus, for the Williams family, and for women's tennis. The twenty-one-year-old had done more than establish herself as the one to beat on the tour. She and Serena had brought African Americans into the sport's royalty for the first time in years. That wasn't lost on those who had come before, including Jeanne Moutoussamy-Ashe, the wife of the late Arthur Ashe, another great African-American player. After Venus and Serena played tennis before a nationwide audience,

Moutoussamy-Ashe sounded as proud as Richard and Oracene Williams.

"I feel tonight the way I'll feel at my daughter's high school and college graduations," Moutoussamy-Ashe said. "Arthur [Ashe] would have liked to have been here for them, because we're all beneficiaries. They've done a wonderful job."

Some might say that things weren't so wonderful for Venus Williams in 2002. She lost her number one ranking to Serena, after her younger sister defeated her in the finals of the U.S. and French Opens and at Wimbledon. But Venus Williams still won seven tournaments and teamed with Serena to win the doubles championships at Wimbledon and the Australian Open. She fashioned a 62–9 record in singles competition and earned $2.5 million in prize money. She may have been "only" number two in the world as 2003 dawned, but she remains a huge force in women's tennis.

And there is more to come—much more. All the hard work and sacrifice have paid off. It's a great time to be Venus Williams.

And the future looks pretty good, too.

stats

Stats

Venus Williams

Born: June 17, 1980
Birthplace: Lynwood, California
Career Titles: 28
Plays: Right-handed
Height: 6' 1/2" (184 cm)
Weight: 169 pounds (76 kg)

Grand Slam Titles:
Wimbledon: 2000, 2001
U.S. Open: 2000, 2001

2002 Tournaments

Tournament	Surface	Round	Opponent	W/L
Australian Women's	Hard	1	Bye	
		2	Patty Schnyder	W
		QF	Ai Sugiyama	W
		SF	Nadia Petrova	W
		F	Justine Henin	W
Australian Open	Hard	1	Ansley Cargill	W
		2	Krisinta Brandi	W
		3	Daniela Hantuchova	W
		4	Magdalena Maleeva	W
		QF	Monica Seles	L
Open Gaz de France	Hard	1	Bye	
		2	Meilen Tu	W
		QF	Silvia Farina Elia	W
		SF	Amelie Mauresmo	W
		F	Jelena Dokic	W
Proximus Diamond	Carpet	1	Bye	
		2	Anna Kournikova	W
		QF	Silvia Farina Elia	W
		SF	Amelie Mauresmo	W
		F	Justine Henin	W
Dubai Women's Open	Hard	1	Bye	
		2	Anna Kournikova	W
		QF	Anastasia Myskina	W
		SF	Sandrine Testud	L
NASDAQ-100 Open	Hard	1	Bye	
		2	Eva Dyrberg	W
		3	Mariana Diaz-Oliva	W
		4	Amanda Coetzer	W
		QF	Elena Dementieva	W
		SF	Serena Williams	L

Tournament	Surface	Round	Opponent	W/L
Bausch & Lomb Championships	Clay	1	Bye	
		2	Amy Frazier	W
		3	Anastasia Myskina	W
		QF	Paola Suarez	W
		SF	Anne Kremer	
		F	Justine Henin	W
Betty Barclay Cup	Clay	1	Bye	
		2	Francesca Schiavone	W
		QF	Arantxa Sanchez-Vicario	W
		SF	Martina Hingis	W
		F	Kim Clijsters	L
French Open	Clay	1	Bianca Lamade	W
		2	Wynne Prakusya	W
		3	Rita Grande	W
		QF	Chanda Rubin	W
		SF	Clarisa Fernandez	W
		F	Serena Williams	L
Wimbledon	Grass	1	Jane O'Donoghue	W
		2	Virginia Ruano Pascual	W
		3	Maureen Drake	W
		4	Lisa Raymond	W
		QF	Elena Likhovtseva	W
		SF	Justine Henin	W
		F	Serena Williams	L
Bank of the West Classic	Hard	1	Bye	
		2	Meghann Shaughnessy	W
		QF	Ana Kournikova	W
		SF	Lisa Raymond	W
		F	Kim Clijsters	W
Acura Classic	Hard	1	Bye	
		2	Janette Husarova	W
		3	Anne Kremer	W
		QF	Kim Clijsters	W
		SF	Lindsay Davenport	W
		F	Jelena Dokic	W
Pilot Pen Tennis	Hard	1	Bye	
		2	Meghann Shaughnessy	W
		QF	Laura Granville	W
		SF	Daniela Hantuchova	W
		F	Lindsay Davenport	W
U.S. Open	Hard	1	Mirijana Lucic	W
		2	Alicia Molik	W
		3	Martina Muller	W
		4	Chanda Rubin	W
		QF	Monica Seles	W
		SF	Amelie Mauresmo	W
		F	Serena Williams	L
Kremlin Cup	Carpet	1	Bye	
		2	Magdalena Maleeva	L
WTS Championships	Hard	1	Patty Schnyder	W
		QF	Monica Seles	W
		SF	Kim Clijsters	L

GLOSSARY

animosity—Ill will or hostility between people.

consecutive—Following in order, without interruption.

controversy—A quarrel or dispute.

cynical—Denying the sincerity of people's motives or actions.

deteriorate—When conditions get worse.

doubles competition—A match between teams made up of two people.

exhibition matches—Competitions that are not directed toward a championship, and are sometimes played for charity.

mainstream—The current or popular trend, thought, or action.

mediocre—Neither very good nor very bad; average.

petty—Small-minded.

prediction—A forecast of how a sporting event will turn out.

prejudice—An unfavorable opinion formed before the facts are known, or despite them.

professional circuit—The collection of competitions involving players who compete for prize money, based on performance.

reign—The period in which a person wins most or all of the time.

seeding the field—A way of ranking tennis players by tournament. Before each competition begins, organizers determine the order in which they think the players will finish. The top seed is expected to have the best chance to win.

surface—The type of court used in a tennis competition. It can be grass, clay, or have a hard, cementlike exterior.

tournament—A competition in which participants are seeded from top to bottom and then pitted against each other with winners of individual matches continuing on until the last two left meet for the championship.

FIND OUT MORE

Books

Christopher, Matt, and Glen South. *On the Court With . . . Venus and Serena Williams.* New York: Little, Brown & Co., 2002.

Gutman, Bill. *Venus and Serena: The Grand Slam Williams Sisters.* New York: Scholastic Paperbooks, 2001.

Morgan, Terri. *Venus and Serena Williams: Grand Slam Sisters.* Minneapolis, MN: Lerner Publishing Group, 2001.

Schimel, Lawrence. *Venus and Serena Williams.* Kansas City, MO: Andrews McMeel Publishing, 2000.

Web Sites

Kids' Zone
Women's History Month
Venus Williams
http://www.usopen.org/bios/ws/wtaw220.htmlThe Official Site of the 2002 U.S. Open

Venus and Serena Williams
http://www/sportsline.com/u/kids/women's/williams_sisters.htm

INDEX

Page numbers in boldface are illustrations.